EASTER EXPLAINED

IN HIS WORDS

FROM JOHN 18 – 21

WALLACE BENN

©WALLACE BENN 2025
ISBN NUMBER 978-1-0369-0982-6
PUBLISHED IN 2025 BY PARKE PUBLICATIONS
COVER DESIGN BY JAMES WT BENN
PRINTED & BOUND BY DANNY RICE, HPS HARDINGS

Unless otherwise indicated, all Scripture quotations are from The ESV Bible
(The Holy Bible, English Standard Version®) copyright ©2001 by Crossway,
a publishing ministry of Good News Publishers. Used by permission.
All rights reserved. (ESV Text edition: 2016)

Scripture quotations taken from The Holy Bible, New International Version® NIV®
Copyright ©1973, 1978, 1984, 2011 by Biblica, Inc.™
Used by permission. All rights reserved worldwide.

Scripture quotations marked NLT are taken from the Holy Bible,
New Living Translation Copyright ©1996, 2004, 2007 by Tyndale House foundation.
Used by permission of Tyndale House Publishers, Inc., Carol Stream, Illinois 60188.
All rights reserved.

Scripture taken from the NEW AMERICAN STANDARD BIBLE®, Copyright ©1960,
1962,1963, 1968, 1971, 1972, 1973, 1975, 1977, 1995 by the Lockman Foundation.
Used by permission.

For Frazer, Bethany & Dexter
(that they may grow to love and follow Jesus too)

With special thanks to my wife Lindsay, and our son, James, whose love and support, as well as editorial, design and type setting skills have been an invaluable help in making this book happen!

PREFACE

These four chapters in John's Gospel are very precious indeed. They are the culmination of John's literary masterpiece bearing witness to Jesus' life, death and resurrection, and they explain the Christian faith in compelling terms. John's own life has been transformed by the knowledge of Jesus, and he wants everybody else to come to that saving faith too (Jn.20:31) His Gospel (or Good News) is the result of mature consideration of all that happened when Jesus came, and is a careful laying out of the evidence as an eye-witness of what took place.

Earlier in his Gospel, John has explained how what Jesus said and did (including a number of miracles) were signposts to who he was (and is) and what he came to do. Now in these chapters (Chs.18-21) he concentrates on the two pillars of the Christian faith – the death and resurrection of the Lord Jesus. They give us the facts as well as explaining the meaning of the events, and show us the transforming effect all this had on the lives of the disciples of Jesus, as well as how it can impact our lives as well.

This little book is a brief commentary on John's writing, emphasising **(in bold type)** what Jesus himself said as a key to understanding what took place, so that you may see the full significance of what he says, and come to know this wonderful Jesus for yourself.

So, please read John's Gospel, or at the least these four key chapters, and come with me on a discovery that may prove as significant for you as it was for John, and me!

(As well as personal use, this book, including the Study Guide at the back, can be used as a six-week Lent Course or Study Course throughout the Year, to help people understand the death and resurrection of the Lord Jesus, and to encourage a personal response to Him in the light of who he is and all he did in love for us.)

WALLACE BENN, EASTER 2025

I

PART I

The Crucifixion

(JOHN 18 & 19)

SESSION I
Who is Jesus and what did he come to do?
(John 18:1-27)

First of all, let us consider *the Context*. John tells us that the events that took place started in a 'garden', where Jesus loved to go with his disciples. Three times in these chapters John mentions a garden (Jn. 18:1,2; 19:41; implied in 20:15). The other Gospel writers emphasise the place, an olive grove called Gethsemane, but John wants us to see the significance of the word he uses.

A Garden

For a Bible student, the word 'garden' reminds us straight away of the Garden of Eden and the beginning of all mankind's problems. It was there that our original parents, Adam and Eve, rebelled against God, deciding they knew better than God how to run their lives. Human beings who inherit the same sinful disposition from our original parents, have all been making the same foolish decision since, seeking to live in God's world without honouring and obeying Him. The pain and chaos of the world shows the results.

John has already begun his Gospel with "In the beginning" echoing the first words of Genesis, to show us that God is doing a whole new work of creation by sending the one who is 'the Word' into the world. This one, identified as Jesus, is God's final word to his world, showing his love and care for those he has made, and his determination to rescue those who listen from the plight they are in. In this garden Jesus is going to reverse the results of mankind's original rebellion against our maker, and make possible a restored relationship with God.

The Passover

The other key word to notice is Passover (Jn.13:1, 18:28). Jesus' crucifixion took place at Passover time. This was highly significant as it is the most important of all the Jewish Festivals.

It celebrates God's greatest redemptive event in their history. How God had delivered his people from slavery in Egypt and set them on the road to the Promised Land. His judgement had fallen on Egypt, but they had escaped because they availed of his means of escape and rescue. They were told to kill a lamb and have a roast supper, putting some blood from the lamb on their doorposts so that when the angel of God's judgement went around he would see the households who believed what God had said for their safety and deliverance, and pass over. John has already told us back at the beginning of his Gospel that Jesus is "the Lamb of God" (Jn.1:36), the one who will carry God's judgement against our sin, in our place. So, John is carefully telling us that in God's perfect timing a new greater deliverance was taking place, through the death of Jesus for us. Caiaphas, the Jewish high-priest had already recognised with a wisdom beyond what he really knew, that someone needed to die *"for the people"* (Jn.18:14).

Anyone wanting to honestly and sincerely investigate the Christian Faith needs to answer two questions: Who is Jesus, really? and What did he come to do? John gives us the answers clearly and succinctly in these verses (18:1-11), and they set the scene to rightly understand the next four chapters of John's account.

1. WHO IS JESUS? – "I AM HE" (18:5,6,8)

When Jesus is arrested by soldiers and officers from the chief priests and Pharisees, he knows all that would happen to him and asks them "Whom do you seek?" When they answer "Jesus of Nazareth" Jesus replies **"I AM he"** (Jn.18:5).

While this is just Jesus boldly identifying that he, not his disciples, is the one they are looking for, it has much greater significance. Jesus literally takes to himself the divine name "I AM" (Exodus 3:14), and as he does so the crowd are bowled over, and fall back (Jn.18:6). It is a display of divine power that shows us who Jesus really is as the Son of God, and it makes it clear that they could not have arrested him without his consent. Despite appearances he is the one in control of events, but he surrenders to them willingly because this is all in

God's plan.

John repeatedly tells us that what happened was in fulfilment of what the Old Testament Scriptures had foretold long before (19:24,28,36). The death of Jesus did not take God by surprise, as some tragic end to an otherwise good life, but rather it was all in God's plan for the salvation of the world.

2. WHAT DID HE COME TO DO?
"SHALL I NOT DRINK THE CUP THAT THE FATHER HAS GIVEN ME?"(18:11)

Undoubtedly Jesus is referring to the awful cup of suffering that lay ahead for him as he was crucified. But it is much more than that. The image of the cup is used in the Old Testament to denote the wrath of God – the cup of God's righteous anger against sin and all that ruins and destroys (see for example, Isaiah 51:17,22; Jeremiah 25:15-29). What Jesus came to do was not just to live an exemplary life, or to show us how to cope with pain and suffering, but supremely to bear the punishment that our sins deserve, in our place.

Peter later states it clearly: "He himself bore our sins in his own body on the tree, that we might die to sin and live to righteousness. By his wounds you have been healed" (I Peter 2:24). That was the real suffering of the cross for Jesus as he became identified with our sin, though himself sinless, and as he carried on his holy shoulders the penalty of our sins.

As the hymn Man of Sorrows puts it:

"In my place condemned he stood,
sealed my pardon with his blood,
Hallelujah, what a Saviour!"

All this, so that we might be forgiven and have a restored relationship with God, knowing his fatherly care and accepted as his children because of what Jesus has done for us. Before the barbarous crucifixion took place, John is telling us why Jesus chose to go ahead and be crucified. It was the only way that God's justice and loving mercy could meet, as God condemned sin and at the same time provided the means of forgiveness. John reveals the very heart of God's love for us in this, that he would send his only Son, who could have stayed in heaven without blame, to achieve that for us!

As we *"Behold the Man!"* (19:5), let us think a bit more about what the rest of this chapter tells us about Jesus, in his own words:

"I have said nothing in secret" (18:20)

Jesus had taught openly and nothing had been done in secret. While Jesus is here reminding Annas of the Jewish law that a prisoner must not be made to testify against himself, but witnesses must be called, he is making it plain that there is nothing esoteric or sinister about what he taught or did. The Christian faith states openly the truth, as we shall see, about ourselves, about God and the world he has made. It tells us about what God is like and how we can have a relationship with him. Everything is verifiable, open and above board!

"Why do you strike me?" (18:23)

Those who knew Jesus well found themselves agreeing with Pilate, the Roman governor, who repeated three times at his trial: "I find no guilt in him" (18:38; 19:4,6). Nobody could legitimately find fault with Jesus in how he lived or what he said and did. His life displayed, here at his arrest and crucifixion as elsewhere, a disregard for his own welfare and a care for others (18:8,9;19:27). The disciples who lived closely with him for three years were unable to point the finger in criticism, something that displays his uniqueness! Come and live with me, or anyone else, for three days and you would reach a different conclusion!

"I when I am lifted up from the earth, will draw all people to myself" (John 12:32)

John has already told us that Jesus said these words long before the event of his crucifixion, "to show by what kind of death he was going to die" (12:33). In this chapter John tells us that

Jesus knew "all that would happen to him" (18:4), and that his earlier prediction was going to be fulfilled as he said it would be (18:32). Despite that special knowledge Jesus had, he showed no hesitation in either "setting his face" to go to Jerusalem, or now allowing his God given destiny to be fulfilled. This shows a remarkable dedication to obey the Father's plan, and also a profound love for those for whom he is about to die.

John paints an accurate and compelling picture of Jesus as the God-man, who is calm in a crisis, powerful and in control of events (despite how it looks), and obedient to God and caring for others even in extremis. Jesus cannot be explained any other way!

3. WHAT MORE DID HE COME TO DO?
(MORE DETAILS EMERGE, AS JESUS EXPLAINS)
"MY KINGDOM IS NOT OF THIS WORLD" (18:36)

Jesus came to establish his kingdom, and bear witness to the truth (18:33-38). Clearly Jesus behaves like a king, with a regal demeanour, which makes a deep impression on Pilate. While admitting that he is a king that has come to establish his kingdom, Jesus is reluctant to say so on Pilate's terms. Pilate is threatened by any talk of a political kingdom that might seek to challenge the power of Rome. But Jesus assures him that his **"kingdom is not of this world"** (18:36).

He is not an earthly king, but is the ruler of what is called elsewhere "the kingdom of heaven" and "an everlasting kingdom". If his kingdom was this worldly he would have called his disciples to arms in the garden, but instead he told Peter to put away his sword (18:36). Jesus rejected the violent establishment of his kingdom, unlike Mohammed, who took the sword in the hope of gaining geographical territory. Jesus' kingdom is amongst those who acknowledge him as the Son of God and the Saviour they need. His rule lasts forever, and will be made manifest when he returns and deals with his enemies at the end of time. He is the supreme king above all kings.

I love the words of the well-known hymn 'The day Thou gavest, Lord is ended' which include the words:

*"So be it Lord, Thy throne shall never,
like earth's proud empires, pass away".*

Earthly empires, however strong, come and go. But to come under the reign of Jesus, to enter his kingdom under his rule and care, is to have eternal peace and security.

Jesus came also **"to bear witness to the truth"** (18:37)

Pilate in his answer to Jesus sounds very post-modern! "Pilate said to him, 'What is truth?'" (18:38). He sounds despairing of ever finding the truth about anything important. Though he is unlikely to have shared the modern dislike of objective truth, which thinks that 'my truth' is as good as 'your truth', which results in a despairing and selfish 'every man for himself' view of life, he certainly felt that truth was hard to find! There are lots of folk like that today! Truth is at a premium in our world!

John has already told us that Jesus taught that "God is spirit, and those who worship him must worship in spirit and in truth" (4:24), that Jesus said that he was "the way, and the truth, and the life" and that "No one comes to the Father except through me" (14:6).

> He is *the way* because as God's Son, he is the uniquely appointed only way to God. He tells us the truth about our world, that it was made by a good and loving creator to whom we are answerable, not by time and chance.
> He tells *the truth* about ourselves as rebel sinners in God's world needing his forgiveness and a restored relationship with him.
> He is *the life* because real life is found in him, not elsewhere, as we discover the reason for which we were made.
> He also gives *eternal/everlasting life* to those who believe and follow him along 'the way'.

Nobody can find the true meaning of life apart from Jesus, or know peace with God without him.

SESSION II
Four reactions to Jesus (John 18:15-19:42)

"Behold your King!" (19:14) The words of Pilate to the crowd can be also used as a reminder to each one of us to really consider who Jesus is and what our response to him should be. Let us think about four different reactions to Jesus, the Saviour and King, in this passage.

1. PETER, THE FEARFUL DISCIPLE (18:25-27)

Peter had been so brave in the garden (18:10), and earlier had said he was willing to die for Jesus (13:37), but now in the courtyard questioned by a servant girl and some folk around the fire, he denied his Lord. Perhaps he was thrown by how quickly circumstances had changed. The disciples had come into Jerusalem with great expectations of the one they had become convinced was the promised Messiah. Now he was arrested, and his life in grave danger. Maybe Peter was just afraid of the personal consequences of being scorned, or arrested, as one of Jesus' disciples – "You also are not one of this man's disciples, are you?" (18:17). He need not have been so scared, the charcoal fire he warmed himself by with others would have given good heat on a cold night but not much light with which to easily recognise him by (14:18). His strong denial "I am not" (18:17,25,27), is in marked contrast to the affirmation of Jesus, **"I AM"**. Peter is outside in the cold in more senses than one!

People can be brave in some circumstances and not in others. Some are physically brave but moral cowards, afraid of what people will think of them. But whatever about us when we behave badly, Peter bitterly regretted this incident. Any unwillingness to stand with Jesus and his followers is always a reason for deep regret in a true disciple! We will later learn of his forgiveness and restoration by Jesus, which is wonderfully told in chapter 21.

2. PILATE, WAS IMPRESSED BY JESUS, BUT FOUND IT TOO COSTLY TO STAND AGAINST THE CROWD.

Pilate found no fault with Jesus, which he says three times (18:38;19:4,6), and tried to release him (19:12), in spite of the baying crowd. But when he is accused by them of not being *"Caesar's friend"** if he releases Jesus, he is afraid of being accused of disloyalty to Rome. His loyalty to his political masters is greater than his concern for justice or truth. His loyalty is earthbound and self-promoting. How sad that he should fail to recognise the one who is the Truth standing in front of him, and to not discover a liberating higher loyalty than to an empire that would one day pass away.

Interestingly, Jesus challenges him as to whether he is responding to him on the hearsay of others or from his own conviction (18:34). Pilate notably becomes more afraid, probably because he senses something of the divine in Jesus (19:7), and is also reminded by him that what authority Pilate has is God given and he is answerable to God as to how he exercises that (19:11). God is in control of the situation, not Pilate!

Many people in our world today are like Pilate. Afraid to stand out from the crowd for truth and justice. Concerned more about their own advancement, and conformity to the political correctness of our day and generation. I well remember someone saying to me after a sermon, 'I do believe that what you say about Jesus is true, but it would be too costly for me and my ambitions to follow him now. I'll think more about it when I am about to die!' He was not too pleased when I reminded him that he did not know when that would be, and that it might be sooner than he thought! The words of Jesus come to mind – *"What will it profit a man if he gains the whole world and forfeits his soul?"* (Matthew 16:26). Pilate let a golden opportunity to do the right thing in relation to Jesus pass him by!

**The title "Caesar's Friend" may have been a title that he got from Caesar through the influence of his patron in Rome, but now that patron had fallen from grace, therefore Pilate's position is less secure, a fact that the Jewish leaders seem now to be exploiting by questioning whether he is really "Caesar's Friend".*

3. THOSE WHO WITH LOVING DEVOTION STOOD BY JESUS (18:15,16; 19:25,26)

The unnamed disciple mentioned in 18:15f, who probably was John himself, seems to have been willing to have been known as a disciple of Jesus, in contrast to Peter who was afraid to be described as *"also"* one (18:17). He is included in the group that remain faithfully standing by the cross (19:26), along with four others including Mary the mother of Jesus, and Mary Magdalene. Their heartache must have been unbearable but their devotion was unmistakable. Their lives, in different ways, had been transformed by Jesus and they are sticking by him with a loving commitment. Nothing would be allowed to shake that. What a good example they are to us!

Notice too, the preponderance of women there at the foot of the cross. Often women's faith and commitment shames us men, for, as someone has remarked, it was women of faith who were the last to leave the cross and the first at the empty tomb!

Two others displayed their devotion to Jesus – Joseph of Arimathea and Nicodemus, both members of the Jewish ruling Sanhedrin, who had dissented from its condemnation of Jesus, but who had been up till now secret disciples (12:42,43). Now they bravely show their true colours by asking for the body of Jesus, burying him in a new tomb owned by one of them, and the other providing a lavish amount of spices with which to anoint the body.

A new tomb in a garden was the sort of place in which kings had been buried, so their kindness is fitting for the King of kings (19:41). The death of Jesus galvanised these wealthy and powerful men, one perhaps representing 'old money' and the other 'new money', to come out in the open clearly as disciples of Jesus. When you come to realise who it is that has been crucified, and what he did for you on the cross, the death of Jesus has the same effect today, leading many to openly profess faith in the Son of God.

4. THOSE, WHO WITH HATRED IN THEIR HEARTS, SHOUTED "CRUCIFY HIM" (19:6,15)

It is a shocking thing to consider how the chief priests and officers led the chorus of "Crucify him, crucify him" (19:6), and how they came through their blind jealousy and hatred of Jesus to deny the essentials of their faith, by claiming that they had "no king but Caesar" in direct contradiction to the second of the 10 Commandments (Exodus 20:3), and the clear statement of Isaiah 43:15, that the LORD alone was to be their king. Their religious position was due to God's grace and goodness, and now God sends his unique Son who stands before them, and they reject him (John 1:11-13). Their fastidious concern with ceremonial purity was in marked contrast to their lack of pure motives as they sought how to rid themselves of Jesus (18:28; 19:31).

The Lord Jesus had seen through their hypocrisy, outsmarted their attempts to trap him by awkward questions, and displayed in his miracles and teaching, as well as in his care for others and his delight in doing his Father's will, a reality of relationship with God that their 'external' religion could not cope with. His integrity threatened them and led them to plot his death. Jewish authorities back then conspired with Gentile civil authority to crucify the Lord of Glory. Jew and Gentile, representing all of humanity, who by our sin have nailed Jesus to the tree.

In the film *"The Passion of the Christ"*, Mel Gibson placed his own hands as the ones that nailed Jesus to the cross. Commenting on this afterwards he said he did that because "It was my sins that nailed him to the cross". That is a profound and true insight, and should be acknowledged by all of us!

It is a sobering thought too, that 'religion' by which people go through the motions but have no personal heart dealing with God, can actually keep us from listening to God and believing in his Son. It can make us feel 'righteous' while never acknowledging that we are sinners who need God's mercy and forgiveness, and coming to trust in Jesus' death alone as the only adequate way our relationship with God can be restored.

We need to ponder too the appalling way that Jesus was treated, by the sham trial at night without witnesses, which was against the law, at which Caiaphas, as the lead figure, had clearly made up his mind already to condemn Jesus. All this compounded by the 'Roman justice' that failed him because of the self-interest of Pilate, who was more concerned about his own position than about justice.

Jesus was beaten twice, the second beating so severe that some actually died in the process, he was mocked, jeered and spat upon and finally crucified (what Cicero called the most barbarous of deaths), yet declared innocent of wrongdoing three times. In the final irony the crowd chose an insurrectionist called "Barabbas" which means son of the father, rather than the true Son of his Father in heaven! (18:40).

God's plan:

Yet John is at pains to show us how every detail of what happened, even in the details of his death, were all in God's plan of salvation, and in fulfilment of Scripture (19:24, 28, 36 – the fulfilment of Psalm 22:1,18; Psalm 34:20; Psalm 69:21; Exodus 12:46 & 1 Corinthians 5:7).

Peter, later expressed this truth well in his sermon on the Day of Pentecost:

> "Men of Israel, hear these words: Jesus of Nazareth, a man attested to you by God with mighty works and wonders and signs God did through him in your midst, as you yourselves know — this Jesus, delivered up according to the definite plan and foreknowledge of God, you crucified and killed by the hands of lawless men. God raised him up, loosing the pangs of death, because it was not possible for him to be held by it."
>
> (ACTS 2:22-24)

SESSION III
What did Jesus Accomplish? (John 19:16-42)

1. HE CREATED A COMMUNITY OF LOVE
"WOMAN BEHOLD YOUR SON! / BEHOLD YOUR MOTHER!" (JOHN 12:27)

There is a very moving scene at the foot of the cross, described for us by John who was himself present (19:25-27). Jesus' selfless care for others is on full display. Despite his own intense suffering, he is concerned for those standing faithfully by him. Mary especially must have felt devastated. There is nothing worse for a parent than to see their child die in front of their eyes, and before their own death. Jesus, whom she had carried and cared for as a child, her very special and unique son, whose birth and life had been so full of hope and joy, now crucified and dying a horrible death. Aware of her pain, and knowing now how much she would need care, Jesus says to her, "Woman behold your son!" and to his "beloved disciple" (John), "Behold your mother".

Mary was probably widowed by this time, and would have depended on her firstborn son for support and protection. That role Jesus now delegates to John, "And from that hour the disciple took her to his own home" (19:27). His selfless love was creating a community of loving care, a family of followers, whose members would try to emulate the care of their Lord by displaying the same kind of selfless care for one another and those who were in need. No believer, Jesus knew, was meant to exist on their own, so he created a fellowship, a church, to provide the necessary support.

Modern people, the surveys tell us, are not only 'anxious' but also very 'lonely', in spite of all the social media, which fails to create real community. Here is Jesus' answer – as we shall see – firstly, the creation of a new relationship with God, and then the creation of a fellowship of believers as our support group to nurture, help and encourage us in the ups and downs of life. What a blessing! And what a reminder to every Christian congregation of believers, how they are meant to relate to one another!

2. HE FINISHED THE WORK THAT GOD THE FATHER HAD SENT HIM TO DO. "IT IS FINISHED" (19:30)

It is always wonderful when an important job gets done! And there is none more important than what Jesus had achieved! Notice the care with which John speaks of Jesus' death. He tells us that Jesus died only when all had been fulfilled that Scripture had predicted, and when he knew that his job of atonement (reconciling God and mankind) had been completed and done (19:28f). His cry, **"It is finished"** is not 'I am finished', but rather a triumphant cry at the end of a job well done! John also observes and carefully notes the reversal of what usually happens. He did not die and his head therefore fall, as would normally be the case, but rather he deliberately "bowed his head and gave up his spirit" (19:30). He willingly gave his life says John, because nobody could have taken it from him had he not willed it to be so. To the very last, Jesus is Lord and in control!

Why crucifixion?

If we are to understand all that Jesus achieved by his death, we must first ask a question – 'Why were the Jewish leaders so adamant that Jesus needed to be crucified?' After all, any kind of death would have got rid of him! But they knew what the Law said, "If a man has committed a crime punishable by death and he is put to death, and you hang him on a tree, his body shall not remain all night on the tree, but you shall bury him the same day, for a hanged man is cursed by God" (Deuteronomy 21:22,23). In their rage, they wanted to show that Jesus was cursed by God because of the kind of death he died.

3. HE TOOK THE CURSE

What they had not grasped was what the apostle Paul so powerfully stated later, "Christ redeemed us from the curse of the law by becoming a curse for us – for it is written, 'Cursed is everyone who is hanged on a tree'" (Galatians 3:13).

Jesus perfectly fulfilled the prediction of the prophet Isaiah, some seven hundred years earlier, as to what the coming messianic Servant would do:

> "Yet it was our weaknesses he carried;
> it was our sorrows that weighed him down.
> And we thought his troubles were a punishment from God,
> a punishment for his own sins!
> But he was pierced for our rebellion,
> crushed for our sins.
> He was beaten so we could be whole.
> He was whipped so we could be healed.
> All of us, like sheep have strayed away.
> We have left God's paths to follow our own.
> Yet the LORD laid on him
> the sins of us all."

(ISAIAH 53:4-6, NLT)

Jesus stood in for us as our perfect sin bearing substitute, taking on his holy shoulders all that God on the Day of Judgement could fairly and legitimately hold against us, for all that we have thought, said and done that has been wrong and has offended a holy God. He carried the penalty of our sin for us, so that we might be forgiven and go free! The word 'tetelestai', translated, "It is finished" was sometimes written on a discharged bill and meant 'Paid in full'. Jesus paid the price in full for our reconciliation with God. He made it possible for us to have a restored relationship with God now, to know his presence and strength through life, and one day inherit heaven with him.

Paul sums it all up brilliantly:

"The life I now live in the flesh I live by faith in the Son of God, *who loved me and gave himself for me*" (Galatians 2:20, italics mine). That amazing love of Jesus for him personally had captured Paul's heart, and it ought to capture ours also!

Another thing needs to be noted. Jesus had really died, and the Roman soldiers who were expert executioners, knew that (19:33). To be absolutely sure they pierced his side with a spear, and John tells us that "at once there came out blood and water" (19:34). This probably means that the spear pierced the heart of Jesus releasing blood and also water from the sack around the heart (pericardium). This is proof positive that Jesus had really died, and that any idea that he was in a coma later to revive is just nonsense.

However, John is also very observant of significant symbolism. He later comments that Jesus came "by water and blood" — probably referring to his ministry which began at his baptism, and his death which was the atonement for our sins (1 John 5:6-8). There he reminds us that God testified to his Son at his baptism, and later by raising him from the dead, to display his approval of all that Jesus' life and death had accomplished.

But water has often been mentioned in his Gospel, symbolising the cleansing and new life that Jesus came to bring. For example: 'On the last day of the feast, the great day, Jesus stood up and cried out, *"If anyone thirsts, let him come to me and drink. Whoever believes in me, as the Scripture has said, 'Out of his heart will flow rivers of living water.'"* And John explains, "Now this he said about the Spirit, whom those who believed in him were to receive" (John 7:37-39). His death made possible the renewing life-giving work of the Holy Spirit in those who open their hearts and lives to Jesus, and trust in all that he has done for them.

From Tragedy to Triumph

In John's Gospel too, the death of Jesus (his blood shed) is not the tragic end of an otherwise great life. Normal biographies end with the death of the subject. Rather it is his crowning glory, for it was for that supreme purpose that he came, to fulfil God's will, and accomplish God's rescue plan for those in the human race who would now turn to his Son.

About his coming death Jesus had said, a short time before,

"The hour has come for the Son of Man to be glorified" (John 12:23). Jesus, as we shall see, was much less the victim of Calvary, and much more the victor!

My daughter, who is a teacher, at one time taught a reception class in which was a particular little boy. He was on an autistic spectrum, and he found socials skills difficult. If he went missing he could usually be found away from the others in the tent in the corner of the classroom, reading. One day they went on a school outing, and were playing in a field. From across the field my daughter heard him shouting, 'Help, Help!' As she looked over she saw him terrified by a large wasp that was circling and threatening him. Jessica shouted across the field, wisely, 'Stay still, I'm coming!' So, she rushed across the field, and when she got near, batted the wasp away. But as she did so the wasp stung her under the arm and she said 'Ouch!' When the wasp had gone, the little boy said to Jessica, 'Do you love me?'. 'Yes' she answered, 'I love all the children in my class'. He replied 'You must love me, because you took the sting for me!'

Jessica later discovered that when he went home he told his Mum, and then everyone important to him by phone, 'My teacher loves me, because she took the sting for me!' The next day when he saw Jessica, he ran up to her, hugged her and said, 'Thank you for taking the sting for me!' At morning break time, his Mum came into school to see Jessica, who was a little worried about what she wanted. But she said to Jessica, 'Thank you so much for what you did for my son, he is a transformed little boy, he now tells everyone that his teacher loves him and took the sting for him!

John tells us in these chapters about a much greater One who took the sting of death for us, because he loved us. That love responded to, will bring about a joyful transformation in our lives too! The apostle Paul wrote, quoting from the prophet Hosea:

"Death is swallowed up in victory.
  O death, where is your victory?
    O death, where is your sting?

The sting of death is sin, and the power of sin is the law. But thanks be to God who gives us the victory through our Lord Jesus Christ."
(I CORINTHIANS 15:54-57)

That's why Christians call the day of Jesus' crucifixion 'Good Friday'!

John was later to write, as an old man,

"To him who loves us and has freed us from our sins by his blood and made us a kingdom, priests to his God and Father, to him be glory and dominion for ever and ever. Amen". (Revelation 1:5,6).

Let us now turn to chapters 20 & 21 to see how the victory of the cross is wonderfully displayed by God raising his Son bodily from the dead.

He committed no sin, neither was deceit found in his mouth. When he was reviled, he did not revile in return; when he suffered, he did not threaten, but continued entrusting himself to him who judges justly. He himself bore our sins in his body on the tree, that we might die to sin and live to righteousness. By his wounds you have been healed.

1 PETER 2:21-25

II

PART II

The Resurrection

(JOHN 20 & 21)

SESSION IV
The fact of the resurrection and the effect on the disciples (John 20)

We now turn to chapters 20 and 21 to see how the victory of the cross is wonderfully displayed by God raising his Son bodily from the dead, and the impact of the Resurrection on the early church.

One of the best proofs of the truth of the resurrection of Jesus is the existence of the church! These chapters show us an initially dispirited and devastated bunch of disciples trying to cope with the death of the one they thought was the God sent Messiah, fearful for their own lives. When John tells us that they huddled together in the Upper Room with the doors securely locked, he is picturing a group locked in on itself! (20:19). As we shall see, they were not expecting Jesus to rise from the dead, as that does not normally happen!

What was it that transformed these disciples into a confident and joyful group, that was willing to risk their lives, for no possible gain – financial or otherwise – to proclaim that Jesus was LORD? Surely no apparition or invention by some of them, would have brought about such a transformation! Only the fact of the resurrection of Jesus, brought about by God the Father vindicating his Son, can explain their new-found excitement and joy! The existence of a daring, joyful and outgoing early church witnesses to the transforming power of meeting with a risen Lord who has conquered death, and lives!

How then did this transformation come about? John is a witness eager to tell us what happened to change everything! Notice the order of events:

1. First, the tomb is discovered to be empty.
2. Jesus appears to Mary Magdalene, (and Peter and John are made to think)
3. Jesus appears to all the disciples, (including a special encounter

for the disciple who was not easily convinced about what had happened)
4. A further meeting with the disciples when they returned home to Galilee.

We will look at the first two in this chapter and the next two in Session 5 & 6.

1. THE EMPTY TOMB – DAYLIGHT DAWNS!

The empty tomb does not of itself prove the resurrection of Jesus, but this fact witnessed to by all the Gospel writers, is the essential basis for a credible belief in a bodily resurrection. A former bishop of Durham, David Jenkins, suggested that it did not matter if someone was to discover the bones of Jesus in a first century tomb, as Jesus lived on spiritually. But that is not the witness of the early disciples, who clearly stated that the tomb was empty and that Jesus was bodily, physically, raised from the dead! Indeed, had this not been true we would have no real hope in the face of death, rather it would be some airy-fairy pipe dream! No, something far more wonderful happened, that gave the disciples transforming hope and joy! Here is John's account of what took place.

2. FROM SADNESS TO JOY! JESUS MEETS MARY MAGDALENE (JOHN 20:1-18)

Mary's deep devotion and the impact of her news on the disciples:
After a no doubt sleepless night, the grieving and traumatised Mary goes to the tomb as early as possible to be sure to be there at first light (20:1). She needed to go to the place where her Lord had been laid, to mourn for the one who had transformed her life (Luke 8:2). To her surprise she finds the huge stone covering the entrance moved away, her assumption being that someone had robbed the grave, to make sad matters even worse! So, she immediately runs and tells Peter and John what has happened, and alarmed by the news they set out running to the tomb, and John, who perhaps is younger (or just fitter!), reaches the grave first. Stooping down to look in (the entrance would not have been more than 3ft.

high) he sees the grave cloths lying but does not go in (20:2-5). Peter arrives, and typically Peter, goes inside and finds the linen grave cloths lying there on the shelf where the body had been, but also notices the head bandage lying neatly folded, separately (20:6,7). John (the other disciple) now looks in and what he sees encourages him to believe (20:8).

Something had happened, and God's fingerprints were all over it! John knew that if the body had been taken, no robbers would have delayed to remove the heavy (with 75 pounds of spice) grave cloths. Anyhow, the spices and linen cloths would have been valuable in themselves, and would have therefore been taken by robbers. If any others had removed the body they would have to have ripped the grave cloths off, leaving a disordered mess, which no disciple would do to expose the broken body of Jesus. When Lazarus was raised he needed help to remove all the grave cloths! (John 11:43,44). Jesus, by contrast, rose from the dead, either most likely passing through the grave clothes or possibly as some have suggested, after laying aside the grave clothes, tidied them up. The scene is one of calm.

John concluded, perhaps a little bit tentatively, that Jesus must have risen! That seed conviction was not yet fully formed or worked through with completely convincing evidence, because neither he nor any of the disciples had digested how Scripture, as well as Jesus himself, had predicted what would happen (20:8,9; see e.g. John 3:14,15; 8:28; 12:23,32; 13:1; Isaiah 53:10). So, no doubt wondering what to make of it all, they returned to their own homes, to report what had taken place (20:10). John would have told Mary, Jesus' mother, who now lived with him, all about it!

Mary's Profound Sadness

As John concentrates on Mary Magdalene's story he does not mention that she had gone to the tomb early with other women, as the other Gospel writers inform us. But John knows about this as Mary's use of *we* in v2 implies.

But now Mary drifts back to the tomb. She wants to be at the last place that she knew Jesus had been. Her grief is inconsolable and initially blinds her to what has happened. At last she looks into the tomb (it would now be light) and she sees two angels seated either side of where Jesus had laid.

Interestingly, they were in the position that cherubim were placed either side of 'the mercy seat' on the top of the ark of the covenant in the Temple, where yearly the high priest made atonement for the sins of the people by sprinkling the blood of a lamb. Jesus the Lamb of God has by his death now made atonement for all our sins once for all.

The angels gently ask Mary "Why are you weeping" (20:13). Even the presence of a vision of angels cannot lift Mary's spirit or quench her grief! Her answer focuses on her distress at the disappearance of the body of Jesus, "They have taken away my Lord, and I do not know where they have laid him" (20:13b). Though dead, he is still her Lord and she wants to finish the burial care of his body, and know he has been safely laid to rest. People in deep grief who have not had a body to bury properly and a grave to attend feel the pain of loss even more deeply.

Mary's overwhelming joy!

But now she turns, hearing a noise or sensing movement behind her, or perhaps, as the great early church preacher John Chrysostom has suggested, she realised someone was behind her by the look of awe in the faces of the angels noticing Jesus! In the glance behind, with tear filled eyes, she neither expected to see Jesus, nor does she therefore recognise him now alive and well! Her head is down in grief not up in expectation.

Jesus gently repeats the question of the angels, **"Woman, why are you weeping?"** There is no need for tears, great news is coming! She replies still looking at the tomb, "Sir, if you have carried him away, tell me where you have laid him, and I will take him away". She assumes she is talking to the gardener, for who else would be there at that time of morning other than the man who had the care of the garden? (20:15). Jesus' second question, **"Whom are you seeking?"** gently raises with her that she is looking for the wrong thing. She is desperately looking for the dead body of Jesus, when she should be looking for a living person, her Saviour and Lord!

Jesus had previously taught his disciples, "I am the good shepherd. I know my own and my own know me" (John 10:14) and "the sheep follow him for they know his voice" (John 10:4) So now Jesus simply says, **"Mary"**. Now she turns giving him her full attention! He knew who she was, and she knew now who he was! So, she addresses him with warmth and devotion, "Rabboni!" in Aramaic, which means something like, "my dear Master" (20:16).

She clings to Jesus, probably his feet, in wonder and worship (Matthew 28:9). Jesus said to her, **"Do not cling to me, for I have not yet ascended to the Father; but go to my brothers and say to them, 'I am ascending to my Father and your Father, to my God and your God'"** (20:17).

Mary was holding on to Jesus lest he disappear again! Jesus assures her that there is plenty of time for him to be with his disciples, 40 days as it turns out, before he ascends back to the Father as the heavenly acclaimed victor over sin and death. Also, Jesus is probably wanting Mary to understand that things will not go back to the way they were. The tense of the verb is present, so in effect he is saying, 'Don't keep clinging to me'; 'it's OK for now but I'm on my way back to heaven, and from now on my relationship with my disciples will be by faith and not by sight'. Notice that Jesus is no ghost or apparition but can be touched physically.

What the atoning death of Jesus further achieved – A new status for the disciples:

Jesus' words also carry a most wonderful explanation of what his death has achieved. Up until now, Jesus had not called his disciples "brothers" – "friends" yes, but not brothers (John 15:13-15). Now because his death has restored his disciples' relationship with God they can be called his brothers in the same heavenly family! The unique relationship between the Father and the Son remains, but they can be part of God's family, knowing his loving care, just as Jesus does!

What overwhelming joy for Mary, and for the disciples! So, hardly able to contain herself, she dashes off to tell them that "I have seen the Lord" and to report what he had said to her (20:18). She has become the first witness to the resurrection of Jesus, and has become the apostle (messenger) to the Apostles!

There is great mercy and love displayed here by Jesus in this event. Women were not thought, at that time, to be reliable witnesses, and could not be witnesses in court. So, for Jesus to choose to reveal himself first to this heartbroken yet devoted disciple, was not only kind in his dealing with her, but also quite counter cultural. As far as Jesus was concerned, Mary was a highly credible witness, as nothing would have brought her lasting consolation other than the fact that Jesus was alive!

Without blurring gender differences or the divine order in family life (and the family of the church), it displays what Paul was later to say, that before God, as far as status and value is concerned, and especially in our relationship with him, "There is neither Jew nor Greek, there is neither slave nor free, there is neither male nor female, for you are all one in Christ Jesus" (Galatians 3:28).*

In Conclusion:

This part of the story shows us a number of things which will become even more plain. The disciples did not expect Jesus to rise from the dead. They were heartbroken, fearful and despondent and nothing could have turned that around other than the wonderful truth that Jesus was alive and had conquered death, and won salvation for them! As they shall see, It was all gloriously true!

---

* By the way, please notice also, that at that time, two male witnesses to the empty tomb, Peter and John, would have been credible witnesses in law to the fact.

SESSION V

From Fear to Faith, with a new Purpose.
Jesus appears to the disciples together (20:19-31).

John does not give us an account of all the resurrection appearances, but is necessarily selective. He does not tell us that other women met with the risen Jesus, nor that he appeared to Peter, nor that he revealed himself to a couple walking along the road to Emmaus on Easter Sunday afternoon (see the other Gospel accounts for more information on these). He now turns from Mary's encounter with the risen Jesus, to how Jesus appeared to the eleven apostles and others in the Upper Room, more than once.

These verses document the crucial appearances of Jesus to the core group of disciples, and are a key factor why the early Christians met to worship on a Sunday. Notice that they were fearful of what the Jewish authorities would do to them, and so locked the doors well, and that they were not at all sure what to make of various reports they were hearing (Mark tells us that they did not believe Mary's account- how could that possibly be true? Mark 16:11). It is to their credit that they stayed together to meet, but they were turned in on themselves in fear and disbelief, and were surprised and taken aback when Jesus appeared in their midst that first Easter Sunday evening.

Assurance:
Jesus said, **"Peace be with you"** (20:19,21,26)

This was a normal Jewish greeting, wishing the disciples well and wanting to quell their fears. But its' triple repetition shows that it was infused with so much more significance now! Jesus' death had accomplished shalom/peace with God for them, in the fullest possible sense. His death had won for them forgiveness of sins and reconciliation with the Father, as well as his victory over death having secured eternal life for them, and for all his disciples. As their Saviour and Lord, he had accomplished what he came to do, and they and all believers would be the beneficiaries! Everything had now changed, and it was time for tears to be gone and delighted joy to take their place!

In his transformed but recognisable resurrection body, Jesus was not prevented by locked doors appearing in their midst! (20:19) But lest they think him a ghost or apparition, he shows them the nail prints in his hands and the spear mark in his side. His scars were visible and touchable, and when they therefore knew that he had physically risen from the dead they were overjoyed and glad (20:20). Luke adds that he ate some broiled fish with them (Luke 24:41-43). Ghosts aren't touchable nor do they eat! Jesus was really alive! It was too wonderful for words, at first! But it was the fulfilment of what he had promised them would happen (16:22).

There is a little connective particle (ouv) in these verses (20:19-31) that is sometimes not translated, but here it is repeated five times and is most helpfully translated as 'so' or 'therefore', as some older translations do (e.g. 20:19, 20, 21, 25, 30 – NASB, quoted below). It is a "marker indicating a conclusion connected with data immediately preceding" (Danker).*

There is a sequence of events here that lead on from one to the other. One is consequent upon the other. If you notice 'so' or 'therefore' (and one 'then'), which I have underlined in the relevant verses, you will see what I mean, and how this brings out the full meaning of the passage.

"So when it was evening, on that day..." (20:19 NASB, my underlining). Jesus had appeared to Mary, and it would not be long therefore before he appeared to the eleven and others, when they had gathered together. "He showed them both his hand and his side. The disciples then rejoiced when they saw the Lord." (20:20 NASB, my underlining).

Frederick William Danker, with Kathryn Krug, The Concise Greek-English Lexicon of the New Testament, The University of Chicago Press, 2009, page 259.

He was not only visible but touch-able and feel-able, therefore he was no ghost but had really physically risen from the dead. Joy unspeakable!

"<u>So</u> Jesus said to them again *'Peace be with you; as the Father has sent me, I also send you'*" (20:21 NASB, my underlining). His death had gained reconciliation and peace with God for all who believe in him. Therefore, they had a mission and a job to preach this good news of forgiveness and eternal life to the world! (20:23,31).

"<u>So</u> the other disciples were saying to him, 'We have seen the Lord!'" ... (20:25 NASB, my underlining). There was no room for doubt, Jesus had indeed risen, and therefore the ten apostles and the others present when Jesus appeared, kept trying to explain to Thomas (who was absent for the first appearance) that the evidence was overwhelming.

"<u>Therefore</u> many other signs Jesus also performed in the presence of the disciples, which are not written in this book; but these have been written that you may believe that Jesus is the Christ, the Son of God; and that by believing you may have life in his name" (20:30,31 NASB, my underlining).

John had to be selective of the many things that Jesus did (20:30), and of the many times he appeared to the disciples after the resurrection, for "He presented himself alive to them after his suffering by many proofs, appearing to them during forty days and speaking about the kingdom of God" (Acts 1:3). But he collected what he had witnessed and had most affected him, so that we too might come to believe in this wonderful living Lord! For the disciples, the ones who had witnessed the appearing of Jesus, they were totally convinced that he had risen. Hallelujah!

Thomas and his doubts (20:24-29).

Let's look in a little more detail at Thomas. Different people deal with sadness in different ways. Thomas appears to have wanted to be alone. But it has been rightly observed that he suffered in sadness longer than necessary because he neglected to meet with the other believers. That is a lesson we all need to learn, "And let us consider how to stir up one another to love and good works, not neglecting to meet together..." (Hebrews 10:24,25).

Nonetheless, thankfully, Thomas was not present when Jesus appeared to the other disciples. I say thankfully, because Thomas' story expresses the doubts of many people with a very rational bent. He was saying in effect 'People who die like I saw that Jesus did, don't rise from the dead. I need to see what the others saw, and even with that I would want to touch the nail-prints and put my hand in the wound on his side to be totally convinced'. "He was downright obstinate" as John Calvin* says. But he too became totally convinced, as a week later, on the following Sunday when they were all together this time, Jesus appeared and invited him to touch and feel as he said he had wanted to do, and see for himself, encouraging him with the words, *"Do not disbelieve, but believe"* (20:27).

The risen Jesus knew what Thomas had thought and said, though not visibly present when he had said it! He met his stubborn objections in a totally convincing way, so Thomas responds with the clearest and greatest statement of faith and worship yet from a disciple, "My Lord and my God" (20:28). It is the culmination of all that John has been trying to tell us in his Gospel, which had started by saying that the disciples had seen the glory of the Word who "was God" and who "became flesh and dwelt among us and we have seen his glory, glory as of the only Son from the Father, full of grace and truth" (John 1:1,14). Thomas has at last got the point and in one fast overtaking move has shot to the top of the class! The resurrection was real and proved that Jesus had conquered death and was to be worshipped as the Son of God, and the Saviour that God's people had longed for, for so long.

---

* *Calvin's Commentaries, The Gospel according to ST JOHN 11-21, Translator – T.H.L.Parker, Wm.B.Eerdmans Publishing Company, 1959, page 209.*

The Equipping and Commissioning of the Disciples:

"Jesus said to them again, '**Peace be with you. As the Father has sent me, even so I am sending you**'. And when he has said this, he breathed on them and said to them, '**Receive the Holy Spirit. If you forgive the sins of any, they are forgiven them; if you withhold forgiveness from any, it is withheld**'" (20:21-23).

The disciples are now sent as witnesses to the resurrection and with a wonderful message to proclaim! They will carry God's authority as they proclaim and live out in a community of love the Gospel of forgiveness and new life, and there will be a special blessing for those who have not themselves seen, but who will believe because of the apostolic witness to what God did in Christ recorded for us in John, and the other books of the New Testament (20:29; see also Luke 24:46-48). John puts it like this elsewhere:

> "That which was from the beginning, which we have heard, which we have seen with our eyes, which we have looked upon and touched with our hands, concerning the word of life – the life was made manifest, and we have seen it, and testify to it and proclaim to you the eternal life, which was with the Father and was made manifest to us – that which we have seen and heard we proclaim also to you, so that you too may have fellowship with us; and indeed our fellowship is with the Father and with his Son Jesus Christ. And we are writing these things so that your joy may be complete"
>
> (I JOHN 1:1-4)

The above verses make it clear that those who have fellowship with the Apostles by believing what they believed and bore witness to, means that as a result they get to have fellowship with God himself also!

Happily, the disciples were not expected to carry out this huge mission to the world in their own strength, but with the help of the Holy Spirit, the Spirit seen in Jesus' life and works, who would not only be with them but in them to enable them to live for Christ, and empower them for witness (14:16,17,26; 15:26,27; 16:7). But the Holy Spirit could not come to them until Jesus had been glorified by his return to heaven. So, Jesus breathes on them, not into them yet, in what my old professor, J. I. Packer, helpfully described as "an acted prophecy".* It was a sort of promissory down-payment on what the disciples would receive fifty days later after Jesus' ascension, on the Day of Pentecost, when the Holy Spirit filled them and empowered them for the task that Jesus had called them to do. A wonderful future God sent prospect, which they would in time experience!

To Sum Up: What did the death and resurrection of Jesus achieve?

- The resurrection and then ascension of Jesus is God's vindication of his Son, of all that he said, did and achieved. It displays him as the living Lord, and not a dead hero!

- Jesus fulfilled God's plan for the salvation for all those who would avail of the rescue package won by Jesus, and given freely to all who believe and trust in him as Saviour, and follow him as Lord.

- We are reminded that the hope and joy of the gospel message is for the whole world, and his disciples have a commission from him to carry out, as they go into all the world in obedience to Jesus, with a love for the otherwise lost who are 'without God and without hope' in his world.

- The Christian Faith is not essentially a religion of do's and dont's, but a personal transforming encounter by faith with the Son of God, "who loved me and gave himself for me" as Paul wrote (Galatians 2:20).

J I Packer, Keep in Step with the Spirit, Crossway, 2005, page 109

Our response to him ought to be the same as Thomas' as we bow in worship and acknowledge him as *"my Lord and my God."* Only then will we experience the forgiveness and new life he has so lovingly won for us.

It ought not to surprise us that if Jesus is who he claimed to be, that God the Father would in a wonderful miraculous way bear witness to his Son by raising him from the dead. For he was sent as Saviour to a world that is in rebellion against its Creator, but loved by him still (3:16), and who calls us back to himself uniquely through his Son. That call must not be sidestepped or ignored, but responded to!

SESSION VI
A wonderful epilogue, bringing encouragement and re-commissioning – John 21

Chapter 20 seems to form a natural end to John's Gospel, and certainly gives us enough to think about to lead us to faith in the Lord Jesus, which is John's stated aim. But there is no manuscript evidence of chapter 21 ever being detached from the rest of the Gospel. So it is better to think of this chapter as a wonderful epilogue in which John cannot resist from telling us what happened afterwards, when the disciples left Jerusalem, when the Feast of Unleavened Bread was over, and they returned to Galilee, as Jesus had told them to do. In God's good providence, we have this precious material we would not have known about from elsewhere. Personally, this is my favourite passage in the whole of the Bible! For excited but shell-shocked disciples, still recovering from the emotional roller coaster of what they had experienced in Jerusalem, what they needed was encouragement about the future direction of their lives now that Jesus had risen from the dead. This meeting with Jesus back home by the shore of the Sea of Galilee provided that for them, and more besides.

Breakfast by the Beach (21:1-14)

Some years ago, when I was leading a tour and staying in Tiberias, I got up very early and went to my favourite place, called Mensa Christi (the Table of Christ), just down from Capernaum. It is almost certainly the place where John 21 took place, as it is near a stream where it is good to catch fish when they are hard to find! In the early morning sun there was a haze on the lake, and about 100 yards out there were fishermen in a boat catching fish. I was able to tell how many were in the boat but could not have recognised a single one had I known them because of the haze. No doubt, had they known me, they would not have recognised me either! This explains why the disciples did not recognise Jesus making breakfast for them on the shore, and it was only the similarity with what Luke recounts happened earlier in Jesus' ministry that prompted John's recognition of Jesus (Luke 5:1-11). This took them back to an early encounter with Jesus when he called them to follow him. Having directed them to catch a big haul of fish, he then promised that from that point onwards they should not be afraid because, "From now on you'll be fishing for people!" (Luke 5:10, NLT).

The disciples had gone back to Galilee, as Jesus had told them to, but did not know when he would appear again. As they were hanging about waiting and wondering what to do next, Peter, their leader still, said, "I am going fishing" and the other six disciples with him replied, "We will go with you" (21:3). For want of something better to do they returned to their old familiar ways.

Jesus said to them:

"Children, do you have any fish?" (21:5)
"Cast the net on the right side of the boat, and you will find some" (21:6)

Like the incident in Luke, though they were experienced fishermen, they caught nothing, until the stranger on the shore, who had inquired as to whether they had been successful, directed them to cast their net on the right side of the boat. As they obeyed him, they caught a huge haul of fish, which they had difficulty in landing on the shore! (21:4-6,8,11). One of the disciples must have counted the catch, because John tells us there were 153 large fish! (21:11).

The lesson for them? Obedience to Jesus brings blessing, and obedience to their original call to "fish for people" was still required, and must remain their priority calling! In the light of Jesus' glorious victory on Easter weekend there could be no going back, they now had a new purpose and a renewed evangelistic calling to fulfil. The incident was also a graphic reminder of what Jesus had earlier said to them, ... *"apart from me you can do nothing"* (15:5).

Let's look at the rest of this chapter under the following six headings, which I have connected with what Jesus said:

1. RESURRECTION

Jesus said to them, **"Come and have breakfast"** (21:12)

I'm always struck by the physicality of this event. Ghosts or apparitions don't prepare and eat breakfast with others, as Jesus does here! His resurrection body was transformed no doubt, but there was no doubt at all that is was Jesus himself who was there with them physically that morning (21:12). Fellowship with the risen Lord has always been the joy of every true Christian believer, but we have to wait to see him face to face till he calls us home to heaven. But on this occasion the disciples had the joy of the risen Lord physically with them at breakfast. He was truly alive and well, and in control of what was happening.

2. REPENTANCE

Peter's encounter with Jesus, while walking along the shore, was profound and life changing (21:15-25). Verse 20 shows us that Jesus had gone for a walk on his own with Peter.

Peter had shown how eager he was to meet with Jesus, after he had been recognised by John, by counter intuitively putting on his fisherman's tunic and jumping into the water to swim/wade to the shore! He had stripped off for work, and he needed to be dressed, not for a swim, but to meet King Jesus! After breakfast Jesus had gone for a walk with Peter along the shore. Peter had unfinished business with his Lord. He needed to deal with the guilt of his threefold denial of Jesus, and he needed to know if Jesus still had a job for him to do as the disciples' natural leader, or had he blown it?

Jesus said to Simon Peter, **"Simon, son of John, do you love me more than these?"** (21:15). Here we see the tenderness of Jesus dealing with Peter privately as they walk together. But we also see the tough but healing love of Jesus. The scene had been set by a charcoal fire. The only other place the word charcoal is used in John was to describe the fire in the courtyard where Peter warmed himself when he denied his Master. No doubt the fire itself would have brought back memories to Peter. But the threefold question directed to Peter by Jesus, **"Do you love me"** hurt him and opened the wound of his threefold denial.

What Jesus is doing is lovingly making Peter face the event that was eating away inside him with guilt. Jesus removes the Elastoplast to let the air at the wound in order for it to heal. The first way that Jesus puts the question, **"Do you love me more than these (other disciples)?"** (v15) makes Peter face the proud self-confidence he had expressed earlier, "I will lay down my life for you" (13:37), which he had not lived up to on the night of denial.

What is so clear in this passage is that Jesus still loves his disciples, wants to be with them to reassure them, and does not hold it against any of them that they all "forsook him and fled". Peter is forgiven, for Jesus went to the Cross for him and the others, knowing full well that they would let him down (13:38). He won God's forgiveness and blessing for them, and for us.

Peter answers Jesus' question with a progression of answers from "Yes, Lord: you know that I love you" (2x,21:15,16) to "Lord, you know everything; you know that I love you" (21:17). Peter knew that Jesus knew everything, from where the fish were that morning to the secrets of people's hearts. To acknowledge that Jesus knew all things, including what the future held for him, as we shall see, was to acknowledge that Jesus was God, who alone knows all things. It was also to feel confident that the Lord knew what the future held for them, and was in sovereign control of it all.

The question of Jesus, **"Do you love me?"** was also important for another reason. Love is the motivation for service, and it is only love that will keep 'doing our duty' from becoming drudgery. All Christian service must begin at the foot of the cross in wonder love and praise when we realise who it was who died for us, what he achieved, and the enormous privilege of being called into his service.

I was reminded that love is the best motive for service when I had a conversation with an older teenager in our youth group some time ago, who told me that he had walked several miles out of his way to carry home the books of the girl he had fallen for in his form at school! Though certainly no fan of extra walking, he told me it was 'no problem' as 'I'm in love!'

3. RESTORATION:

He said to him, **"Feed my lambs"** (21:15,16,17)

The fact that Peter's past failure was forgiven and dealt with is reinforced by Jesus giving him a job to do, and repeating it three times to counteract his threefold denial! He still wants him to fulfil his calling and role, by feeding (teaching) and pastoring (caring for) all his "sheep", that is those who follow Him as the Good Shepherd (10:11), whether they are big or small (lambs or sheep)! That is a role that Peter took seriously for the rest of his life, and shared it with other overseers/under shepherds who were called to teach and pastor all the followers of Christ too (I Peter 5:1-4). Jesus knew that the health of the church depended on leaders who would, after the unique role of the Apostles as witnesses to all that God had done in Jesus, be "pastors and teachers" to carry on that aspect of Apostolic ministry in building up the church.

4. RECONSTRUCTION:

"Jesus said, **"When you are old you will stretch out your hands"** (21:18)

No doubt the disciples wondered what the future held for them. By Jesus telling Peter about his future martyrdom (tradition tells us Peter was crucified upside down in Rome during the Neronian persecution of Christians, circa 65 A.D.) he assures him that he knows what will take place and that the future is in his hands. What happens to believers will be a matter of what is in accordance with his will for them (21:22). That was a tough call for Peter, but his death would glorify God, and not be wasted (21:19).

We can face the future if we know it is in our Saviour's tender hands, and that he will be with us giving us his help in life's journey, and that he will finally take us safely home (Matthew 28:18-20; John 14:3). I remember asking a strident young atheist, who had debated with me in a sixth form class, but who had later become a Christian, what the difference was between living as an atheist and living as a Christian. "That's easy", he replied in a flash, "The presence of Jesus with me makes a world of difference!"

5. REALISATION:

Jesus said, **"Follow me"** (21:19)

There is a cost in following Jesus and Peter is made to face that squarely by his Lord. Jesus calls all his disciples, *"If anyone would come after me, let him deny himself and take up his cross and follow me"* (Mark 8:34). That does not mean martyrdom for many of us, but it will involve sacrifice, and it does mean laying aside our selfish agendas and seeking to go God's way as we follow his Son, who knows what is best for us. However, the benefits of knowing and following Jesus is what Paul later called of such "surpassing worth", that everything else is rubbish by comparison! (Philippians 3:8). For as Jesus himself put it, *"What does it profit a man to gain the whole world and forfeit his soul?"* (Mark 8:36).

Peter had another lesson to learn from Jesus, that is so important for us all to learn. We often can see how God's truth should be taken on board and affect others, but are not so quick to see how it applies to ourselves! I remember as a young Curate hearing a brilliant sermon by my boss on the misuse of the tongue. The biggest gossip in the Church shook his hand warmly on the way out of church saying, 'That is just what Mrs Brown needed to hear'!

Peter wants to know what Jesus has in store for his close friend, John, whom he notices has been following them as they walked. Jesus says in effect, 'I may or may not grant him a long life, if that is my will for him, but what is that to you? You need to concentrate on following me, no second guessing my will for others. Trust me to do what is best for them' (21:20-23). Note too that John uses the present tense to record what Jesus said, which means, *"Keep on following me"*. Peter's somewhat erratic behaviour formerly was now to be a thing of the past, and Jesus is calling him, and us, to have some consistency about our discipleship. We are called not to be discipleship sprinters, like Usain Bolt, but to be long distance runners like Mo Farah!

6. REASSURANCE:

"Jesus said to him, '**If it is my will that he remain until I come, what is that to you? You follow me!**'" (21:22)

The Lord has all things in his hands and he wants Peter to follow him and fulfil the job he has for him to do. As the risen Lord he says *"All authority in heaven and earth has been given to me. Go therefore and make disciples..."* (Matthew 28:18,19). He is also "head over all things for the church" (Ephesians 1:22,23, NIV), and he can be trusted to use his authority for the good and blessing of his church, for Peter, and for all those who come to know and follow him as Saviour and Lord.

Peter must have remembered now with deep gratitude what Jesus had said earlier to him, "Simon, Simon, behold, Satan demanded to have you, that he might sift you like wheat, but I have prayed for you that your faith may not fail. And when you have turned again, strengthen your brothers" (Luke 22:31,32). The Good Shepherd never loses one of his sheep for he said, "I give them eternal life, and they will never perish, and no one will snatch them out of my hand" (John 10:28). And he ever lives to make helpful intercession for us now (Hebrews 7:25). Peter and the others were safe in his everlasting hands. Peter now more than ever wants to strengthen the others and fulfil his calling for his Lord!

As we move towards a conclusion of our study together, two more things need to be said:

Firstly, what we have been reading in John is an eyewitness account of what he knew to be true. Others among the apostolic group also stood with him in bearing witness to the fact that what the "beloved disciple" had written is indeed true (21:24).

Secondly, John reminds us that he had to be selective in what he wrote, as the words and acts of Jesus were so many and wonderful! Indeed, what he said and did, and all that he achieved, is of truly infinite value, and stands head and shoulders above anything else you will find in any library! (21:25).

In Conclusion:

The call of this loving and living King Jesus, who died and rose to bring forgiveness and eternal life to us, and to all those who respond in repentance and faith to him, is as real today as it was for Peter when he said to him, **"Follow Me"**.

Jesus asks each one of us three potentially life changing questions, in the light of who he is, and what he has done for us:

1. Do you love me?

2. Will you follow me?

3. Will you serve me and bear witness to me?

So how about it? What is your response?

Some suggestions to find out more about Jesus:

'Two ways to live' booklet: *http://twowaystolive.com/*
'Christianity Explored': *www.christianityexplored.org*

Blessed be the God and Father of our Lord Jesus Christ! According to His great mercy, he has caused us to be born again to a living hope through the resurrection of Jesus Christ from the dead, to an inheritance that is imperishable, undefiled, and unfading, kept in heaven for you, who by God's power are being guarded through faith for a salvation ready to be revealed in the last time. In this you rejoice...

1 PETER 1:3-6

A SELECT BIBLIOGRAPHY

Andreas J. Kostenberger
John, Zondervan Illustrated Bible Backgrounds Commentary, 2002

James M. Hamilton Jr.
John, ESV Expository Commentary Vol. IX, Crossway, 2019

Rodney A. Whitacre
John, IVP New Testament Commentary, IVP, 1999

D.A.Carson
The Gospel According to John, IVP Pillar Commentary, 1991

Karen H. Jobes
John Through Old Testament Eyes, Kregel Academic, 2021

Leon Morris
Expository Reflections on the Gospel of John, Baker Book House, 1991

John, W. Hall Harris
in 'The Bible Knowledge Word Study' on The Gospels, Editor: Eugene H. Merrill, Victor (Cook), 2002

J. I. Packer & Mark Dever
'In my place condemned He stood', Crossway, 2007

Marcus L. Loane
'Jesus Himself'– the Story of the Resurrection, The Banner of Truth Trust, 2007

James Montgomery Boice & Philip Graham Ryken
'14 Words from Jesus', Christian Focus, 2013

STUDY GUIDE

Questions for Discussion: Six Sessions on John 18–21.
Please re-read the relevant passages.

SESSION I
Who is Jesus and what did he come to do? (John 18:1-27)

1. What is significant about a 'garden' (18:1; 19:41)? How is the 'Passover' (18:39) a suitable setting for Jesus' death?

2. Consider the bravery of Jesus in self-identifying himself and taking the attention of the arresting soldiers away from his disciples who might have been arrested too? (18:8,9: 17:12)

3. What does the arrest of Jesus tell us about (a) who he is (18:5,6), and (b) what he came to do? (18:11)

4. What do you make of Peter's action and Jesus' response? (18:10-11) What does this tell you about the nature of Jesus' kingship?

5. Who was Caiaphas? What dangers do religious authorities face? Why did he say what he did and what is its significance? (18:14)

6. In his response to Annas (who had been High Priest but was deposed by the Romans, but was still held in esteem by the Jews), what do we learn about Jesus himself? (18:23; 18:32 c.f. 12:32) And what do we learn about how he conducted his ministry? (18:20,21)

SESSION II
Four reactions to Jesus – *Which one is like you?* (John 18:15-19:42)

1. Why was Peter so brave earlier and so cowardly in the courtyard? When are we like Peter?

2. Note in this passage the attempts of Pilate to release Jesus, and his conclusion about his guilt. Why did Pilate fail, and what caused him to buckle and give in? Do we see any of Pilate in us?

3. Jesus was a King, and acted like a king, and had authority. But what was different about his kingship and his kingdom? (18:36) What does Jesus before Pilate tell us about him, and also about Jesus?

4. Jesus came to bear witness to the truth (18:37). What is the truth he is referring to? Why is truth so important? (John 14:6). What has happened in our world to devalue truth? Do we devalue it? If so, how?

5. Why were the Jewish authorities so adamant that Jesus was crucified? (19:6) Why is the substitutionary nature of Jesus' death so important? (Galatians 2:20; 3:13).

6. What does devotion to Jesus by those at the foot of the cross, and his care for them, show us? (19:26,27; 13:35).

SESSION III
What did Jesus accomplish? (19:16-42)

1. The story of the Crucifixion of Jesus is told in seven incidents, verses 17-18; 19-22; 23-24; 25-27; 28-29; 30; 31-37. How does each incident show us some aspect of the glory of Jesus?

2. Ponder the significance of each word that Jesus said from the cross (19:26,27; 19:30).

3. How was the Scripture fulfilled in the death of Jesus, and why was that important? (19:24,28,36).

4. What is the significance of the blood and water that flowed from Jesus' side? (I John 5:6-12).

5. What made Joseph of Arimathea and Nicodemus now come out in the open as disciples of Jesus. What hinders us sometimes in being openly seen as disciples of Jesus?

6. Think about what Peter later wrote about the Crucifixion and what Jesus achieved (I Peter 2:21-25). In what ways does John agree with what Peter says?

SESSION IV
The fact of the Resurrection and the effect on Mary, Peter and John (John 20:1-18)

1. Why was Mary so sad? Why was the empty tomb not enough to bring joy?

2. Why did she not recognise who was standing behind her? Why does she try to hold on to Jesus? What does that signal about a change in how Jesus would relate to his disciples from now on?

3. Peter and John witnessed the empty tomb. Why is that important? What did John notice that made him believe? (20:8). What is significant about what Jesus told Mary to tell to the disciples? (20:17).

4. What does the way that Jesus dealt with Mary tell us about Jesus, our King? What does it tell us also about the nature of his resurrection? (20:17)

5. In what ways is Mary an example to us?

SESSION V
Jesus appears to the disciples, and the effect upon them (John 20:19-31)

1. Why were the disciples slow to believe that Jesus had risen? How were they feeling? What convinced them that he was really bodily present with them? Compare the same incident in John 20 and Luke 24:36ff. What extra do we learn from Luke?

2. What was especially important about what Jesus said and did in the Upper room? Why does Jesus repeat, "Peace be with you" three times? How does one thing flow consequentially on to the next? What does Jesus breathing on them signify?

3. Thomas' story is a great help to us. How? What did Jesus say and do to help Thomas? Why is Thomas' response so important? What extra blessing is promised by Jesus and how does that affect us?

4. What was the effect of witnessing a risen Lord upon the disciples? How did Jesus recommission them, and what help in witnessing to him did he make? When was that promise fulfilled? (vs 20-23).

5. How would you witness to someone sceptical about the reality of the resurrection today?

SESSION VI
A wonderful epilogue bringing encouragement and re-commissioning (John 21)

1. Why was the breakfast with Jesus back in Galilee so important? What memories did it evoke, and why were they important? (see Luke 5). What does it tell us about Jesus? What further proof does it give us of the reality of Jesus' physical resurrection? What does it tell us about the disciples? How were they helped by meeting again with Jesus?

2. Why was it so important for Peter to have a private conversation with Jesus? What was his greatest need? What do we learn from the attitude of Jesus towards Peter? (For personal reflection and action – what is troubling us that we need to talk with Jesus about?)

3. Why does Jesus ask Peter, "Do you love me" three times? Why was this especially difficult for Peter. Think about the tender tough love of Jesus in this story, and how it can be mirrored in our lives? Why is love so important to any service we are involved in?

4. Peter is reinstated by Jesus as the leader of the group with a particular responsibility. What was that? And how is that discharged in our church today? (I Peter 5:1-4) As Jesus had prayed for Peter do we pray enough for our leaders and seek to support them?

5. How did Peter seek to distract attention away from his following Jesus, by asking about John's future? Do we ever do the same? Have you counted the cost, as well as the joy and privilege of following Jesus? If not why not?

6. Why can we trust what John has written in his Gospel? (21:24). What is the aim that John had in writing his Gospel? (20:30,31). What effect has this Gospel, and these chapters in particular, had on you individually and as a group?

— WALLACE BENN, EASTER 2025

ALSO AVAILABLE

The "Last Word"

JESUS' TEACHING IN THE UPPER ROOM

WALLACE BENN

"When the head and the heart and the passions of the expositor are fully engaged in opening the biblical text, a fine commentary will result – that is what this book is."

R. KENT HUGHES